Great African-American Artists Coloring & Activity Book

by

Alicia L. McDaniel

This book is dedicated to my mother Beverly and my elementary school art teacher, Mr. A. Crute. Thanks for believing in and nurturing my creative potential.

This book may not be reproduced in whole or in part in any form, or by any means, electronic, mechanical, recording or otherwise without written consent from the author/publisher.
Published by Alicia McDaniel Fine Art in conjunction with
Art For the Creative Soul

Great African-American Artists Coloring & Activity Book
by Alicia L. McDaniel © All Rights Reserved
ISBN 978-0-9891824-3-0

About the Author

Alicia L. McDaniel is a professional artist, creative author and educator. With over 16 years of experience as an art educator, she has worked with students from ages 5-65. Her mission is to create and offer exciting, yet affordable multi-cultural art lessons/activities inspired by amazing artists of color. Visit www.aliciamcdanielfineart.com and www.artforthecreativesoul.com to learn more about her.

Artists featured in this book

Basquiat, Jean-Michel
Bearden, Romare
Burke, Selma
Catlett, Elizabeth
Douglas, Aaron
Evans, Minnie
Fuller, Meta Warrick
Hunter, Clementine
Johnson, Sargent Claude
Jones, Lois Mailou
Lawrence, Gwendolyn Knight
Lawrence, Jacob
Lewis, Edmonia
Palmer, Hayden
Pippin, Horace
Powers, Harriet
Ringgold, Faith
Savage, Augusta
Smith, Hughie Lee
Tanner, Henry Ossawa
Thomas, Alma
Waring, Laura Wheeler
White, Charles
Wilson, Ellis
Woodruff, Hale

Each artist featured in this resource has a portrait-coloring sheet, biographical information and a set of questions connected to a simple art activity. Each set of questions or activity has a cross-curricular connection. Use the legend below to determine which cross-curricular connection goes with each set of questions and/or activity.

Careers/Technology	☐
ELA (English Language Arts	☑
Math	✚
Music	♪
Physical Education	O
Science	❖
Social Studies	✪

Tips for Using this Resource

This resource can be used for students in grades K-12. Visit www.artforthecreativesoul.com to print or download free examples of the artists work. While the questions are designed for children in grades 5-12, you can use them to start discussions with younger students. Moreover, feel free to tailor the questions to fit any age level. Each art activity can be completed with simple art tools. In addition to coloring the artist portrait coloring sheets, answering the questions and completing the art activities, the list below contains several more ideas for using this resource.

- ➢ Color the artists portrait sheets using a monochromatic color scheme.

- ➢ Write words that describe the style, art or life of a specific artist to fill in the artist portrait coloring sheets and/or frame.

- ➢ Use various textures to color in each artist portrait sheet, such as pointillism, cross-hatching, lines, or torn pieces of colored paper.

- ➢ Use various mediums to add color to the artist portrait coloring sheets.

- ➢ Use the artist portrait coloring sheets to develop drawing skills by creating blind contour drawings or upside down portrait drawings.

- ➢ Use each individual artist as an "Artist of the Week" or month and feature them on a bulletin board.

Contents

Harriet Powers	5
Henry Ossawa Tanner	7
Edmonia "Wildfire" Lewis	9
Aaron Douglas	11
Augusta Savage	13
Horace Pippin	15
Minnie Evans	17
Sargent Claude Johnson	19
Selma Burke	21
Hale Woodruff	23
Meta Vaux Warrick Fuller	25
Ellis Wilson	27
Clementine Hunter	29
Palmer Hayden	31
Laura Wheeler Waring	33
Romare Bearden	35
Gwendolyn Knight Lawrence	37
Jacob Lawrence	39
Lois Mailou Jones	41
Hughie Lee Smith	43
Alma Thomas	45
Charles White	47
Elizabeth Catlett	49
Jean-Michel Basquiat	51

Harriet Powers
1837-1910

Harriet Powers was born in Athens, Georgia. She was a folk artist who created beautiful quilts. Harriet's work displays a traditional style of American quilting. She combined traditional African appliqué techniques with European record-keeping and biblical references to create the stories displayed on her quilts. Harriet's quilts were first exhibited in 1886. Her work is on display at the Smithsonian in Washington, DC.

☑✪ **Answer each question with a complete sentence.**

1. List two different forms of fiber art.

2. What do you think about Harriet's quilts?

3. Describe your favorite quilt or blanket.

✚ **Create an original quilt design by adding drawings or patterns to the squares.**

Harriet Powers

Henry Ossawa Tanner
1859-1937

Born in Pittsburg, PA, Henry O. Tanner was one of the first African-American artists to receive international recognition. Henry became passionate about art at a young age and began painting at the age of thirteen. Mr. Tanner taught art at Clark University in Atlanta, GA for a short period of time. Furthermore, he attended the Pennsylvania Academy of Art and studied art in Paris where he lived most of his adult life. While, Mr. Tanner painted many religious scenes, one of his most famous paintings is entitled *The Banjo Lesson*.

☑♪ **Answer each question with a complete sentence.**

1. *The Banjo Lesson* depicts an older man teaching a young boy how to play a banjo. What instrument do you play or would like to learn how to play?

2. List three elements of design.

3. Who is your favorite artist? Why?

♪ **Design a banjo or guitar by completing the drawing below. Add color to your drawing.**

Henry O. Tanner

Edmonia "Wildfire" Lewis
c.1844-1907

Edmonia "Wildfire" Lewis' family heritage consists of Native-American and African origins. After the unfortunate passing of both of her parents, her Native-American aunts adopted her and raised her on a Chippewa reservation in the Buffalo, NY area. She attended Oberlin College in Ohio for a short time and later developed her sculptural ability under the tutelage of a professional artist. Edmonia created her most well known sculptures while living abroad in Rome, Italy. Her beautiful sculpture celebrates the beauty of figures of African origin as well as other ethnicities.

☑❂ **Answer each question with a complete sentence.**

1. What is the difference between a sculpture and a drawing?

2. How do you think growing up on a Native-American reservation influenced Edmonia's art?

3. Why do you think her nickname was Wildfire? What is your nickname?

✣ **Turn the circle into a sphere by shading it. Include a highlight and shadow**

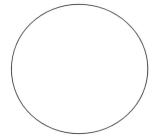

Edmonia "Wildfire" Lewis

Aaron Douglas
1899-1979

Aaron Douglas was born in Topeka, KS on May 26. His mother enjoyed painting, which influenced Aaron at a young age to become interested in art. He graduated from the University of Nebraska with a bachelor degree in fine arts. Aaron relocated to New York City in 1925 and married educator, Alta Sawyer. As an artistic leader during the Harlem Renaissance, his home became a meeting place for many prominent African-Americans such as Langston Hughes and W.E.B. Dubois. He was also a graphic artist for the NAACP magazine and taught at Fisk University for 27 years.

☑Answer each question with a complete sentence.

1. Do you have a family member or friend who is an artist? What kind of art do they create?

2. What would you like to study when you go to college?

3. Aaron painted many images inspired by his African-American heritage. What is your favorite subject to paint or draw?

Draw a simple sketch of your favorite subject to draw.

Aaron Douglas

Augusta Savage
1892-1962

Augusta Savage was an acclaimed artist who studied sculpture in Europe. Born in Florida, she was also an activist and educator who was one of the leading artist of the Harlem Renaissance. As a child she began creating sculptures out of natural clay. Augusta studied sculpture in New York where she lived for most of her life. After winning a Rosenwald Fellowship, she went to Paris and exhibited at the prestigious Grand Palais. Mrs. Savage helped to establish the Works Progress Administration for artists of color and created the renowned sculpture entitled *The Harp*.

☑⊙Answer each question with a complete sentence.

1. What kind of tools are best used to create a sculpture using clay?

2. Define the word *prestigious*.

3. Augusta was an educator and an artist. How did her ability as an artist help her as an art educator?

Draw a picture of your favorite tool to create art.

Augusta Savage

Horace Pippin
1888-1946

Horace Pippin was a self-taught artist who was born in Westchester, Pennsylvania. He did many drawings during his childhood. Horace enlisted in the United States Army in 1917. Unfortunately, he lost use of his arm after being injured in World War I. Pippin used a long tool to hold up his injured arm and began painting once he returned home. Painting was therapeutic. Horace was married and had one son. He took art classes when he was older and experienced at least three solo art exhibitions during his lifetime.

☑ **Answer each question with a complete sentence.**

1. Creating art is great way to relax. How do you feel when you create art?

2. Horace was a self-taught artist. List one thing you have taught yourself.

3. What are three details that an artists needs to include in a work of art to ensure that it is complete?

❖ **Horace used oil paint to create his work. Use oil pastels to color the flower below.**

Horace Pippin

Minnie Evans
1892-1987

Minnie Evans was a folk artist who was born in Long Creek, North Carolina. She was only able to attend school up to the sixth grade. Minnie married her husband in 1908, had three sons and lived on the property of her husband's employer for many years. One night she had a dream, which inspired her to create a drawing with pen and ink. Evans continued to create art inspired by her dreams and the natural beauty of her surroundings. She had her first formal art exhibition in Wilmington, North Carolina in 1961 and went on to become a celebrated artist.

☑❖**Answer each question with a complete sentence.**

1. Describe one interesting detail from your most recent dream.

2. Minnie was inspired by nature and her dreams to create art. What inspires you to create art?

3. What do you think about her work?

Color and decorate the butterfly below.

Minnie Evans

Sargent Claude Johnson
1888-1967

Sculptor, painter, and graphic designer Sargent Claude Johnson was born in Boston, MA. His family heritage consists of Native-American, African-American and Swedish ethnicities. As a child, Sargent lived in a variety of places, including with his aunt, who was a professional sculptor. Sargent was influenced by his aunt and later studied art at in California for several years. Sargent became nationally known while exhibiting various works of art with the Harmon Foundation.

☑ **Answer each question with a complete sentence.**

1. Graphic designers create logos, package designs and many other types of designs. What is your favorite logo? Why?

2. Sargent had a diverse background. How does that relate to his artistic expression?

3. List one unique quality about his artwork.

☐ **Design a box for a new brand of cereal that you create.**

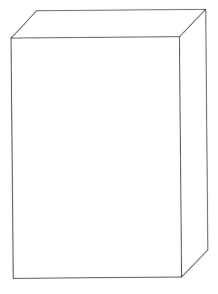

Sargent Claude Johnson

Selma Burke
1900-1995

Selma Burke was a sculptor, educator, and mentor. She was born in Mooresville, North Carolina and graduated as a nurse in 1924. While Selma found a nursing job in Harlem, NY, the Harlem Renaissance heavily influenced her. For many years, she dreamed of becoming an artist and began sculpting in her free time at the Harlem Arts Community Center. After receiving the Rosenwald grant, she studied sculpture in Vienna. Selma Burke has the distinction of creating the bas-relief sculpture of President Franklin D. Roosevelt that inspired the obverse seen on the U.S. dime.

☑ ☐ ✪ **Answer each question with a complete sentence.**

1. What is a mentor? Do you have a mentor? If so, what is their name?

2. List one fact about the Harlem Renaissance.

3. Selma studied nursing and art. Which job is more important, being a nurse or an artist? Explain.

✚ **Create a new coin by designing both sides. Give each coin a monetary value.**

Selma Burke

Hale Woodruff
1900-1980

Muralist, Hale Woodruff, was born in Illinois but grew up in Nashville, TN. He studied art at the Jon Herron Art Institute in Indianapolis as well as at the Chicago Institute of Art. Additionally he studied art at Harvard University. In 1936, he further developed his craft by studying under renowned muralist, Diego Rivera in Mexico. Mr. Woodruff was also an educator who taught at schools such as Atlanta University and New York University. His most famous murals depicting the historic events on the Amistad are on display at Talladega College in Alabama.

☑ ✪ **Answer each question with a complete sentence.**

1. A muralist paints large scenes on a _____.

2. Discuss the similarities and differences between Woodruff's murals and Rivera's murals?

3. Why is it important to commemorate history through art?

Design a mural that could be painted on a wall in your school or classroom by creating a thumbnail sketch in the box below. Add color to the sketch.

Hale Woodruff

Meta Vaux Warrick Fuller
1877-1968

Award winning artist, Meta V. W. Fuller, was born to a middle class family in Philadelphia, PA. She was fortunate to receive training in the arts as well as horseback riding while being encouraged to develop cultural intelligence. Meta won a scholarship and studied sculpture at the Pennsylvania Museum and School of Industrial Art. After graduating from college, she studied art in Paris and became a protégé of Rodin. Also a poet, she was friends with W.E.B Dubois and Henry O. Tanner. Even though she experienced many challenges during her career, she is renowned for her extraordinary talent as an artist.

☑☉ **Answer each question with a complete sentence.**

1. Meta learned how to ride a horse at an early age. Have you gone horseback riding before? When and where?

2. How are Meta's sculptures similar to Rodin's sculptures?

3. She overcame many obstacles in her life. What is the best way to deal with a challenging situation?

❖ **Draw a simple picture of a horse inside the frame.**

Meta Vaux Warrick Fuller

Ellis Wilson
1899-1977

Born in Mayfield, KY Ellis Wilson was influenced by his father who was an amateur artist. He studied art at the Chicago Art Institute. Ellis moved to Harlem, NY in 1928 and worked at a variety of places including a brokerage house and a factory that produced engines. He developed his artistic ability while working for the WPA arts project and later received a Guggenheim Fellowship in which he traveled around the U.S. *The Funeral Procession* is the title of one of his most famous works of art.

☑✪ **Answer each question with a complete sentence.**

1. Ellis was hired to do many different types of jobs. Do you think this fact influenced his art? How?

2. What is the difference between an amateur and a professional artist?

3. Ellis learned a lot from traveling around the United States. What is something interesting that you have learned while traveling?

✪ **Draw a simple picture of your favorite way to travel.**

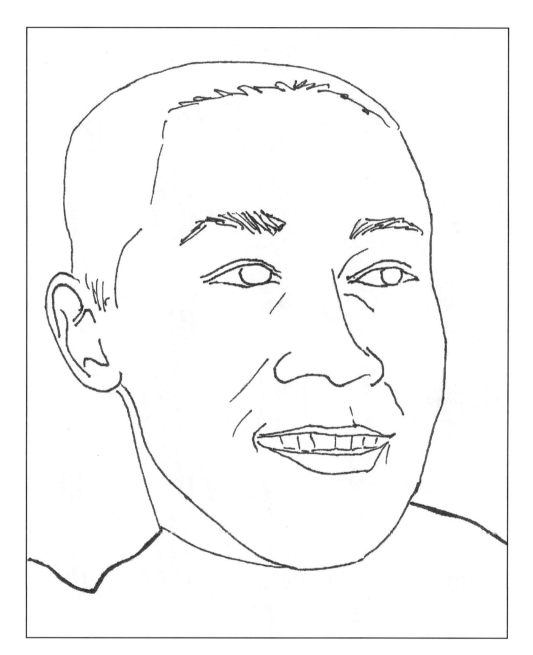

Ellis Wilson

Clementine Hunter
c. 1887-1988

Folk artist Clementine Hunter is known for her colorful depictions of farm life. Born in Louisiana, Clementine married Emmanuel Hunter in 1924 and worked as a field hand and housekeeper for many years. After a visiting artist left art materials at the plantation on which she worked, she used the tools to begin painting. Clementine's art was influenced by her life on the farm. She created over 5,000 paintings and was recognized by two U.S. presidents.

☑❖ **Answer each question with a complete sentence.**

1. Clementine began painting when she was older. What message can we learn from her?

2. Clementine worked on a farm. Have you ever visited a farm? When and where?

3. A picture of land is called a _____.

❖ **Draw a simple picture of your favorite animal.**

Clementine Hunter

Palmer Hayden
1893-1973

Palmer Hayden was born in Wide Water, Virginia and began to draw landscapes as a boy. Palmer joined the United States army and was stationed in the Philippines. After serving in the army, he moved to Greenwich Village in New York where he was hired to do many types of part-time jobs while pursuing a career as an artist. While Palmer studied art at the Cooper Union in New York he is considered to be a self-taught artist. Palmer enjoyed working with both watercolor and oil paint as he focused on capturing the African-American experience in the United States.

☑✪ **Answer each question with a complete sentence.**

1. List one difference between watercolor paint and oil paint.

2. Palmer served in the military. Do you have a family member who serves in the military? What branch of the military do they serve in?

3. Palmer also enjoyed painting seascapes. Do you think his travels around the world influenced his art? Why?

Draw a picture of all of the tools an artist needs to complete a painting.

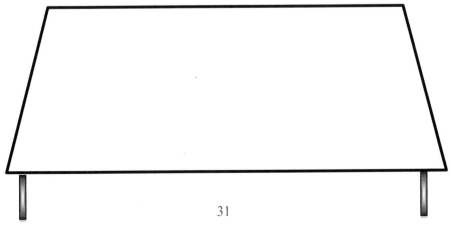

Palmer Hayden

Laura Wheeler Waring
1887-1948

NAACP member, Laura Wheeler Waring, was born in Hartford, Connecticut. Laura's mother was a teacher and amateur artist while her father was a minister. She became a part-time art teacher while studying art at the Pennsylvania Academy of Art. Moreover, she visited Europe to study art after receiving a scholarship. Her artistic contributions also include creating pen and ink illustrations for the *Crisis* magazine. Laura painted many prominent African-Americans, including opera singer, Marian Anderson and former NAACP leader, James Weldon Johnson.

☑ ♪ **Answer each question with a complete sentence.**

1. Marian Anderson was a great opera singer. How is opera music different from other styles of music?

2. What is the difference between a painted portrait and a photographed portrait?

3. What grade were you in when you had your favorite school portrait taken?

♪ **Draw a simple portrait of your favorite singer.**

Laura Wheeler Waring

Romare Bearden
1911-1988

Celebrated artist, Romare Bearden was born in Charlotte, NC on September 2. While he graduated from New York University with a degree in education, he took many art classes, was an art director and created cartoons for various student publications. In 1935, Romare studied art in Paris and later became a member of the Harlem Artists Guild. Romare worked as a social worker for nearly 30 years in New York while he worked on his art in the evening and on weekends. The award-winning artist was married in 1954 and had great friendships with other prominent African-Americans such as Jacob Lawrence and Duke Ellington. Romare created art with various mediums, but is best known for his beautiful collages that depict African-American life and jazz music.

☑**Answer each question with a complete sentence.**

1. What is a collage?

2. How do you think Romare's work as a social worker inspired his art?

3. List one African-American who inspires you? Why?

♪ **Draw a simple picture of the instrument that makes your favorite sound.**

Romare Bearden

Gwendolyn Knight Lawrence
1913-2005

Gwendolyn Knight Lawrence was born in Bridgetown, Barbados on May 26 and moved to the United States at a young age. She attended Howard University and was a student of renowned artist, Lois Mailou Jones. She also studied art with the talented artist, Augusta Savage. Gwendolyn taught dance classes, worked in a library and served on many cultural committees throughout the years. The award-winning artist was married to Jacob Lawrence and began exhibiting her work in the 1960's.

☑**Answer each question with a complete sentence.**

1. Gwendolyn was fortunate to study art with talented artists. List a talented person that you would like to study with?

2. List three principles of design.

3. How is Gwendolyn's art similar to her husband, Jacob Lawrence's work? How is it different?

Gwendolyn enjoyed working with children. Draw a picture of you favorite fictional child character from a book, television show or movie.

Gwendolyn Knight Lawrence

Jacob Lawrence
1917-2000

Jacob Lawrence is respected as one of the most prolific African-American artists of the 20th century. He was born on September 7 in Atlantic City, NJ and spent his early childhood in Pennsylvania. Jacob was about thirteen when his family moved to Harlem, NY. Jacob began drawing and was mentored by a famous African-American artist named, Charles Alston. Jacob developed his love of art into a life-long career. He painted scenes of African-American life using gouache and tempera paint. He also loved and collected all kinds of tools. Throughout his career, he won many awards and his work is displayed around the United States. Jacob was married to Gwendolyn Knight who was also a talented artist.

☑O Answer each question with a complete sentence.

1. What is gouache paint?

2. Jacob painted a series of paintings inspired by the Olympics. What is your favorite Olympic sport? Why?

3. Describe your favorite art tool?

**☐ Jacob used vivid colors to create his paintings.
Use bright colors to design and color your own postage stamp.**

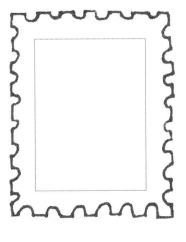

Lois Mailou Jones
1905-1998

Lois Mailou Jones was born in Boston, MA and was inspired by her father's tenacity to graduate from law school. After showing an interest in art at an early age, she went on to study art at the High School of Practical Arts in Boston. Further, Lois graduated from the School of the Museum of Fine Arts. Throughout the years she traveled to various places such as France and Africa, which influenced her paintings. Lois has the distinction of being invited to the White house eight times. She taught at Howard University for many years.

☑✚ **Answer each question with a complete sentence.**

1. Lois believed in supporting international artists. Why is it important to support other people?

2. There are many colorful patterns in several of Mailou's paintings. Define the word *pattern*.

3. Is there another country you would like to travel to that you have never visited before? Which country and why?

✪ **Draw the flag of the country you would like to visit.**

Lois Mailou Jones

Hughie Lee Smith
1915-1999

Hughie Lee Smith was born in Eustis, Florida and moved to Cleveland, OH at the age of ten years old. He had the opportunity to go to art classes at the Cleveland Museum of Art. Meanwhile, Mr. Smith graduated from Wayne State University with a B.A. degree. Also a teacher and performer, he won top prize for his art in 1953 from the prestigious Detroit Institute of Arts. Mr. Smith moved to New York and taught art for over a decade. His art is described as surreal and is on display in art museums around the United States.

☑✪ **Answer each question with a complete sentence.**

1. Define the word *surreal*.

2. What is the "best" art museum you have visited or would like to visit? Why?

3. Describe the range of colors Hughie used in his artwork.

Color one paint palette with warm colors and the other palette with cool colors.

Hughie Lee Smith

Alma Thomas
1891-1978

Born in Columbus, GA on September 22, Alma Thomas was the first fine arts student at Howard University. When she was younger, her family focused on the importance of education and relocated the family to Washington D.C. in 1906. Alma took her first art classes at Armstrong Technical High School. She graduated from college with a degree in fine arts. Moreover, she earned a M.A. degree in art education and taught art for many years. She began displaying her beautiful abstract art after she retired from teaching.

☑✪Answer each question with a complete sentence.

1. How did Alma use light and dark colors in her art?

2. Have you relocated from one neighborhood, city or state to another? What is the difference between where you once lived and where you live now?

3. Do you like abstract art or realistic art? Explain.

Draw a simple picture of your neighborhood.

Alma Thomas

Charles White
1918-1979

Charles White was born in Chicago, Illinois. He was a talented artist who contributed to the Works Progress Administration. Charles created beautiful lithographs and drawings that were exhibited at the Smithsonian and the Chicago Institute of Art. Moreover, one of his most well known murals is on display at Howard University and depicts renowned African-Americans. He taught art the Otis Art Institute from 1965-1979.

☑**Answer each question with a complete sentence.**

1. Charles White created beautiful portraits. A portrait is a picture of _____.

2. How is printmaking different from drawing?

3. What is your favorite tool to draw a portrait with?

Draw a simple portrait of one of your favorite family members.

Charles White

Elizabeth Catlett
1915-2012

While Elizabeth Catlett was born in Washington D.C., she lived most of her adult life in Mexico. She graduated cum laude with a B.S. degree from Howard University. Additionally, she studied under famous artist Grant Wood at Iowa University and graduated with a masters of fine arts degree. After marrying Mexican artist, Frances Mora, she moved to Mexico. The prolific sculptor, printmaker, professor and activist created powerful images of oppressed people.

☑ **Answer each question with a complete sentence.**

1. How does art reflect culture?

2. List one fact you have learned about Mexican culture?

3. How is the process of printmaking different from the process of sculpting?

Draw a thumbnail sketch of a sculpture that could be used to decorate the school.

Elizabeth Catlett

Jean-Michel Basquiat
1960-1988

Self-taught artist Jean-Michel Basquiat was born in Brooklyn, NY on December 22. His mother took him to major art museums around New York City when he was a young child. Jean-Michel started his career by painting images on T-shirts. Meanwhile, Jean-Michel used his artistic ability while working for a clothing company. He went on to become an internationally known abstract artist. Basquiat collaborated and was close friends with famed artist, Andy Warhol.

☑ **Answer each question with a complete sentence.**

1. Basquiat was a self-taught artist. How do you express yourself through art?

2. Why is it important to visit art museums and galleries?

3. What can you learn by collaborating with other artists?

☐ **Create a colorful t-shirt design.**

Dr. Faith Ringgold
1930-

Native New Yorker, Dr. Faith Ringgold, graduated from City College. She is an award winning artist, professor, curator and author who is also known for her hand-painted quilts. While Dr. Ringgold has associated with many prominent artists throughout her career, she mentors and encourages emerging artists. As the founder of the *Anyone Can Fly* non-profit foundation, she has authored over 16 books including one of her most beloved books entitled *Tar Beach*.

☑ Answer each question with a complete sentence.

1. Compare Faith Ringgolds' quilts to Harriet Powers' quilts. How are they similar and different?

2. Faith Ringgold is an award-winning artist. List an award you have received and explain why you received it.

3. What is the title of your favorite book? Why is it your favorite book?

Draw a simple illustration of a scene in your favorite book.

Faith Ringgold

Make sure to also purchase *Great Art Lessons for the Creative Soul* by Alicia L. McDaniel. This exciting art lesson book compliments *Great African-American Artists Coloring & Activity Book* and is inspired by 11 prominent African-American artists.

The book features:

- ➢ Step-by-Step Colored Photos
- ➢ Lesson Templates
- ➢ A Concise Glossary
- ➢ Cross-Curricular Connections
- ➢ Discussion Questions

Visit www.artforthecreativesoul.com to purchase this resource as well as find additional art lessons, activities and free examples of the artist images.

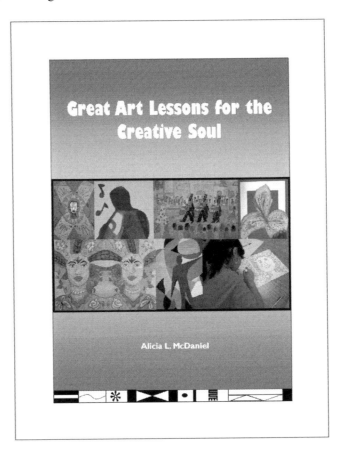

Made in the USA
Columbia, SC
16 April 2023

15090495R00033